Only Looking For Jewels

icon303

Only Looking For Jewels

Dedicated to:

Dad,
May the lines drawn
Guide you to a place
Of true happiness.

Only Looking For Jewels

Only Looking For Jewels

Only Looking For Jewels

Published by Coyote Blood Press
& Paradisiac Publishing.

Cover Art by icon303

ISBN: 9798712369973

www.icon303.com
IG: @icon303
Twitter: @yugo_icon303

Only Looking For Jewels

Only Looking For Jewels

icon303

Only Looking For Jewels

"*The most important places*

on a map are the places we

haven't been yet."

-The Map of Salt and Stars
By Jennifer Zeynab Joukhadar

Keepsake

Foreshadowing is
~~Meaningless~~

And all but behind
The chirping echoes
Of the Beast
That scared
Even the Beast.

What else is there
When the moon
Sets in new waves
Over a warm volcano,

Or the smoldering coals
Beneath us resonates upward,
Besides a cool, calm collective

That can make everything a

keepsake?

Broken Spanish aside,
I'm already tasting
The Goya in the air
And can hear
The plantains falling.

I told you this would happen.
Now I only have one request:
If you ever come visit,
Bring a shovel
And bury me
Right here.

The Seed

Incarnation of
And much like
The love and respect
That bind us,

You are the ropes
That tether me
To this universe...

Without you
I'd be lost in space
With the rest of the
Celestial beings
That lost their
Love.

Jamais Vu

And there I was,
31 and still fighting the
Demons strolling down
My cheeks, laying in
Fetal position on my
Bedroom floor;

Squeezing the Beast's
Extra fur as I sobbed.

I thanked her,
In case I don't survive this,
For all she's done
Over the last 7 years.
Times haven't been
The best they could,

But squeezing her

Extra fur eased it all.

I'll never let go.

Anoles

Take a stroll with me,
And glide over the tiny,
Prehistoric world beneath.

Smile at those you pass,
For they understand
The exact same as you.

Take a stroll with me
Away from your past;
They can't catch up
If we don't ever sleep.

Smile at the waves crashed,
For they understand
The exact path as you.

Take a stroll with me

To the voodoo man
That has chicken bones;
He has a wicked recipe
For madmen like us.

8567-8529

Despite this hellish watering hole
A magic winter did a sauntering roll
And was exactly what I needed
To know my role
I may stop by every few months or so
When my feelings get low
Help me elevate my soul

Let each dying brain cell
Beget the honor of a falling star;
A decaying supernova
Ready to Prometheus a new
Universe upon its demise.

I walk slowly as to not stir
Any air into gusts of ripples.

Goddamn Hamlet

Am I a comedian, or a poet?
I don't fuckin know either.
Isn't comedy just poetry
With a punchline?
Isn't comedy how you season
The food in poetry's lunch line?

You May Never Know Me

The marble and granite
Are almost lost on me now
Because of the DGK loving,
Drug dealing hustler
I once was.

A couple of dabs hits
And documentaries about
Graffiti can soothe my soul.
It gives it a way
To communicate
With the universe,
If you let it.
Montana has to make up
Viable percentages of my
Blood stream by now.

I can be in Ecuador
And see a piece
And instantly smell
And taste the Bronx
And know I'm part
Of a beautiful,
Multicultural,
Artistic revolution.

I have something to say
And your building looks like
The perfect marquis.

Call the Police

There hasn't been
        a day you haven't

Crossed my mind,

And a week
        I haven't cried

Since I gave you my last hug

At the top
        of that stairwell.

Underside

There's poop
On the underside
Of the table,
And I just stuck
My foot in it.

I think the ants
Put it there
Because I ate
Their last mango.

Anyways, ass cheeks
Are bare for a frozen drink.

Want me to bring
The sign in?
I don't know
If the weather

Has my mother
On speed dial yet,

But there's sand
In the waters.

Boomshakalaka
I want purple
In my belly.

Lost Child

He didn't know

     what he was looking for,

But he never went home.

Cumwash

I'll still be here,
Unanswered texts
And all.
Doest thou
Quench thy thirst
Or art thou
Insatiable still?
Earnest not
Whilst mobbith,
My liege.

Something Named Desire

Go, bitch.
Clock is ticking.
Come again.
Bye.

Past Haints Haunt

Is someone else there?
If not, then what was that
Sound from the kitchen?

I know you're there!
So, show yourself,
You fucking coward!

Is someone else there?
If not, who is going to
Hear it when I fall down?

I know you're there!
So, hold out your arms
And catch me, asshole!

Is someone else there?
If not, why did that

Haunting shadow move?

I know you're there!
So, come out! Show me
Your hands, haint!

Thank You
Right Back

Text gangbang orgy
You swinging, publishing,
Big-dick author.

Death by a million
Thank you's to you.

I wish I could
Smush your poetry
With my face

Life by a million
I love you's.
Tool marks showed
The way out
To a table of

Zoo-house dominos
Holding kangaroo court.

Rodney Hit It First

A solum drive
Into Vero exposed
Fields of green
With only palms
Sticking up in
Sparse slaloms out of
Sandy turf.

This place was
Waiting for us.
It's the perfect escape
For a writer.

There were 7 guns
In the car
And 700 rounds
Of varying caliber,
All ready to be shot

At the range.

Who wants to put money
On how fast we can shoot them off?

Maybe an hour before
We're on the road
To the beach.
Everything here was
Quiet, peaceful.
Something I've sought
Since arriving.

Everyone at the beach was
Disobeying direct orders
From the government,
But who could pass up
The sand and surf;
Even the sun made its way.

The beach was perfect
With a light breeze
And beautiful, tranquil waves
To put our minds at rest.
Water perfect green
And sand as white as
The snowbirds still stuck here

During quarantine.

Only a Sandbuffalo
Would sleep through this
With flies flying
Around his eyes.

She

Ran to the door
Like someone was running
Right behind her.

You have to say goodbye
No matter how
Hard that may be.

Push out the
Words that paralyzed
Your tongue cold.
Fight past the tears
That will fall
For years in memories.

"I can't say it,"
She squeals hyperventilating,
"Goodbye!"

Tears propelled themselves
Downward
In mass succession,
Knowing it was
Going to be the last time
Soulmates hugged.

Nirvana

Nobody loves icon303.
I wish I could buy a mold
Of your heart to sleep in.

Beast of Beasts

For the thousandth night
                    in a row,
I woke you up before we both
                    headed off to sleep.

Back-to-back,
Or you in my arms,
Or your face pressed against mine,
Or nose snug under my chin;

Protecting my throat
                    while we sleep
Because a true protector's job
                    is never done.
What a shining gem you are.

Hidden in
the Hills

You've still got my heart
      in a cherry chest,

I know it.

You say you lost it, but

I bet if you unpacked
      your closet,

You'd find it there,

Barely beating next to an old
      sundress and shelltoes,

Under the gun.

Just leave it be.

Hath the Highway

Only looking for jewels,
May haste hath the
Highway there.

Come and sit down with us,
Pull up a chair and have a smoke.

The pebbles on the sidewalk
Might point you westward,
But we all know your heart
Is seeking refuge on an island.

Somewhere,
Only looking for jewels,
With a clock ticking
Posthumously
In the background.

The water rings might bind
My hands to a less fortunate
Timeline before it all could
Finally deteriorate without

Permission.

Passed over

They've told me
I'm wise beyond my years
But as the years churn,
I feel like maybe
I was smart in the old ways.
In the old world.

Bow to the Audience

Oh, leaves.
In the carpet
I lay

A string, a string
Straitens up the
Ant's mound.

Goodbye, boyo.
From the bilge,
We fold.

Hey Dad,

Yesterday was the Beast's birthday,
And today we're on our way
      to Port St. Lucie.

Sandbuffalo put on
Toad and The Wet Sprocket
      without knowing the

Connection as we smoked a joint
On the way to Jensen Beach.

The beach was perfect,
Waves crashing chronologically
One more joint before I
      jump in a rip current
      because both can carry me
      to another world.

Lay out on my towel
With sand covering
The back of my head.

Close my eyes and listen
To the waves crash,
The wind,

The Sandbuffalo and Ilene Suttonfuse
                    laughing while
                    collecting shells.

I heard they had an
          oyster place close by,
          let's bring our
          craziness there and feast.

The waitresses were kind
And beautiful,
The food was delicious,
And fresh,
The people were laughing,
And enjoying their drinks.

I couldn't help
But look around

And think,
"And they say the
World is ending."

Last Look

Before I Left

Is a picture of a picture
Worth a million words?
And when I see it
Will my mind
Be filled with fanfare?

If I could go back,
I'd shower your little face
With kisses more often
And tell you
How proud I am.

If I could go back,
I'd tell you
I love you more
And never let the hugs go.

If I could go back,
I'd take you away
From it all
And never look back.

Just Babies

Just babies
The Beast and I were
Just a few years ago.

Bury us deep
Beneath the fishing poles
And boardwalk.

I Write

Cop found a Xanax on me
But yeah, that's for me
I suffer from PTSD,

And I'm dead broke,
And don't know how
The public assistance works
For mental illness.

I don't have the money
To spend the time in lines,
Or filling out more applications,
Or meeting new counselors
At a new meeting
To get turned down from.

That's part of the illness too,
The constant rejection,

Fear of abandonment…

And so, I write.
I write and I write
Until my hands fall off.
I write until the wrongs are right
I write until everything is alright.

Succumb

Psychedelics have survived
Just as long
As the Torah.

Which makes them
Just as real
As your gods,
Maybe even more so…

And just as worthy
Of worship and praise.

Rose and Amber

Your love lies
In Florida skies.

Shirtless Oatmeal

Thinking back
To a time when
I could laugh
At everything.

Maybe I just
Haven't experienced
Enough

And that's why
Everything was
So new and entertaining.

And maybe it's because
Now I've been through
So much that it all
Seems insensitive to

Joke about.

I'm sorry.

Time Pause

We're already dead,
Our deaths chosen
Like a stopwatch
In the tide.
Maybe yours is
A grandfather clock,
Or a cuckoo.
Maybe analog,
Or digital.
But our time of death
Is already out there,
Waiting for us
To catch up.

Red or Blue?

There you were near
The cash register when I
Walked in with my hood up.
The way you looked at me
Was like you knew that
Yugo has a way of
Changing people's lives
When he walks into them.

He has a way of introducing
The little bits of chaos
That spin off into their own
Little beautiful galaxies of life.
Alice didn't know she was lost
Until she fell into the hole.
Which one are you going to take?
The red pill or blue pill?

And now Alice brings
Different colored pills
To all the white rabbits of the forest.
All because she was standing
Near the cash register
When Yugo walked in
With his hood up and
A mind full of acid.

Brick-and-Mortar

What came first?
The shadow or the light?

Sometimes your day ones
Are the ones putting
The knife in your back.
Sometimes they are the ones to
Leave you with less than
They found you with.

What came first?
The friendship or the fight?

Sometimes you're closed in
And the ones closed out
Will never understand why.
Sometimes they are the ones
That are the reason for

Your brick-and-mortaring.

But what would they know
About how to treat you
When they haven't learned
How to treat themselves?

Black Widow Woman

There you were,
Right in my shoe.
I guess I should've
Looked before I stuck
My foot in there.

There's probably
                    more of you, too.

Under the couch
And behind my towel,
Where I plug in my phone
And in the blankets.

There you were,
To take it all away
Like I owed you something.
Guess I should've

Looked before I stuck
My hand in there.

There's probably
            more of you, too.

Next to the spent bullet casing
And in the box of cereal,
Above my head on the ceiling
And behind the cabinet door.

There you were,
Right in their ear,
Telling them you'd
Get them anyways.
I guess they should've
Looked before they stuck
Their heads in there.

There's probably
            more of you, too.

Current

You're just drifting
A little too far
From the shore
And a rip tide
Is at your heels.
Just swim
And let the yells
Fade off
Into the distance.
There is no
Saving you now.

Prometheus

Quarantine has been kind
To a rambler's only dream
To write and describe
The world around him
And pour it into silicone molds
To pop them out 24-hours later.
It's been kind to dreams and
Searching deep within one's self
To find what makes them happy.

For me it's much more simple
Than most other's dreams.
Give me a pen and a piece of paper
And I'll write you a symphony,
Draw you a Sistine Chapel,
Color in the shades of my love for you
Outside of the lines and in
An astounding spectrum of hues.

I just need to create.

I didn't need quarantine to do it,
Just needed a reason to isolate.

Dec. 19ᵗʰ, 2019

My birthday is usually
Just another day to me,
But you gave me a bigger gift
Than I expected when we went to
El Torito for dinner that night.

Everything was perfect.
Your hair was perfectly curly
And eyes gleaming with how
Excited you were to
Take me to dinner.
It was so cute and so appreciated.

I ordered my drink,
And you ordered yours,
And they came pretty fast
Despite how busy it was.

But why did he
Serve it with his left?

Maybe he's just new, I thought.
The deeper we got into conversation,
The less we noticed the
Things around us.

The waiter came back,
We ordered our food,
And dove right back in
Until the appetizers came
And he served them with his left.

The table next to us
Needed the next round of drinks
And when they came,
I watched his hands
And saw why he served with his left.

I saw why he wore long sleeves
In South Florida heat,
And why he was better
Than his coworkers,
And it told me more than
I ever thought about him.

He came and took our plates
In a single trip and brought us
Our desert immediately.
We promptly devoured
The entire thing,
Even licking up
The left-over syrup.
And when he brought us the bill,
He delivered it with his left.

This time I knew why.
I knew about the
Teasing his coworkers must do
And how much harder his boss
Must ride him than everyone else.
I knew about the self-consciousness
And need to be better other people.
I knew about the nights in bed
He must've asked why.

So, when you paid the $50 tab,
I left a $65 dollar tip
Because he served with his left.

And he'll never know that I knew,
He'll never see me again to ask.
I just wanted to do something

That will give him
A different reason
To ask why

And you bringing me
To a place to be able to do that
Was the greatest gift
I've ever got.

Northern-Most

Is there a
Northern-most lizard,
Or is there a latitude
That the lizards
Just don't cross?
I must know.

Yesterday Happened

It's been a long time
Since yesterday happened.
So many things
Have happened since.
I almost forgot it happened
Until I came home
To an empty house and silence.
It's only been 24-hours,
But it feels like a lifetime
Since you called it quits.
Let's hope it only takes
24 more to forget it altogether.
It's just been so long
Since yesterday happened
I can't believe it was
Just yesterday.
But it was and
You're still gone

And I'm still here
Waiting for it to be over.
Hit me with something heavy
And knock the memory loose
So I can move on
To tomorrow.

Wheels on the Bus

Ignorance is see-through.
We can all see your
Wheels turning
Trying to do the math.

We can see the smoke
Billowing out of your ears
Trying to solve the riddle.

If it wasn't so sad,
It would be the funniest sight.
This is the result of trying
To keep bloodlines pure
And the people submissive.

I'm just thankful I've always
Colored outside the lines
With no fear.

It's nice and roomy where
No one else dare settle.
This is home.

Bass Drop

The frequency has
Changed around here.
It's gotten quite cold
And the hertz has
Dropped dramatically.

I wish life had a way
To increase the volume
Past that of which it is.
That's possibly just my need
To push things to the edge.

All kinds of things
I've exhausted trying to find
The point where I fall off
And let gravity take the wheel.
The scariest part is:
I still haven't found anything

That looks close…

But you can be sure
That when I do,
I'll waltz somewhere close
With something I hold dear.

Curly's

I still remember
When you had
The whole family
Gather in the parking lot
Of the restaurant
Where I cooked
To sign off
On me being
Unwittingly taken out
Of my grandparent's will.

Morning Hair

You were so beautiful
         with your morning hair

Glowing in the sun
         breaking through the shades

The Beatles

Pissing in the wind
Pissing in the wind
The hammock flaps
And random trash
Littered through the hood
Pissing in the wind

Queenberry Thickett

I haven't seen you in so long,
It's good to see you write.

Your gaze is so strong
It may take all of the night
To completely learn
What the last year has done,
What joy has burned,
What sadness was fun.

I know later this week
You'll be with him again
And I've thought of
Being alone, instead.

But if it's better to have
Loved and lost
Then this must feel like winning.

Because most I've loved
And then lost;
Sold my love at cost.
You were the only one
Who meant, "I love you."

That's why
I shoved you
Away.

Sand Angels

The beach ills me
And pulls me further
From society.

Leave me here
On a sand dune
In the sun
And problems
At my back.

The old life
Is no longer
Such an abusive
Paramore anymore,
And I'm no more
Its faithful victim.

I've fallen for UVs

And the taste
Of salt water.

Bring Us Out

Things are getting restless here.
Sounds of gunfire outside and
Dogs barking at ghosts.

There were smoke signals
Sent into the sky for you,
Did you receive?

You're twelve minutes late
To your own damn party.
Water has run out so
We're switching to whiskey
Despite the CDC advising
Against any notion that
Would bring us out of
Misery.

Fill me with love

And then leave…
Fuck it,

You might as well
Kill me
While we're practicing

Destruction.

Strongman Contest

Popped my head over the fence
To say hi to my neighbors.
Mike is a good man;
His roommates are terrible, though.

I had to ask about the kid
Across the street who got shot
Last week and about the roommate
Of his I shot at last month.

Everything is calm now
And the kid across the street
Was set up for good reason.

But the best news was Mike
Is in good health finally.
Prostate cancer takes
The hardest of men

And he's in remission.

I could've jumped through
The fence and hugged him.
What great news
For a rainy afternoon.

Queensboro

I'll remember everything
About this day:

Green top with blue jeans.
You ordered Chardonnay
At a brewery
And blessed me
With knowing Belly.

You gave me great feelings
About times ahead
And you didn't know it.

Toiled Delicacy

Somebody fucking
Toiled for that,

Somebody's fucking
Hands bled for that.

Yet, there she was,
Sitting in a long sweater;

Sipping coffee out of my heart
As she held it with both of her

Delicate hands.

Doorhole

Tell the door to get keyed,

I've got your fuckin smile.
Look at me now, ear to ear.

The door is right there,
Go whisper what I told you.

Don't be such a pussy
And say it like a man.

Get. Keyed.
Take the brass deep within.
No WD-40, no spit,
And a lot of missed attempts.

Heh, by the time you're 50,
Your keyhole will look like

Wombats launched an assault.

We'll have to grind down the metal
And polish it with sandpaper,
So, don't flinch.

Come on, go tell it.
We don't have all day.
Just let whatever terrible words
You wish you could say to someone;
Berate the door in front of you.
Punch it.
Kick it.

It's the only thing holding you back.

So, what's stopping you from,
At the very fuckin least,
A good ol' tongue lashing?
Do you still have balls?

Or just sit there,
You fuck.

Just Above
Our Heads

Spiders are
Plotting our deaths
From the spackled ceiling.

Don't ever stop
Jumping fences
Because they'll
Always be
6 legs ahead.

Good thing geckos have 20 toes
And translucent skin and a hunger
            for the insanely creepy.

Gobble, sticky-tongue, gobble.

And please excuse my voyeurism,
But I fancy your work,
My good friend.
And those
Colors are cool.
Do you like weed?
Can I have
Your autograph
On my tits?

I'm never
Washing these again,
I swear it.

Who Won?

Silver lining:

My roommate
Placing bets
On the 2020
Presidential debates.

Train Station

There's a textured
                yellow ledge…

Don't you dare
        step across it.

There are spiders
And snakes
And sharp,
Jagged rocks
To catch
Every last
Bit of your dignity.

Why can't the crackhead
Be Like the homeless man
On the bench over there,

                        asleep.

Not hurting anyone comes
With a long list of very specific
Reasons in the yellow ledge;

Look at all the reasons
Bubbled up so you
Don't lose your
                footing.

I Said

What I Said

If there is a *god*,
He or she
Definitely made
Two things right:

Women and words.

Old Me

I am
Who I am;

Accept,
Or move on
        without
                me.

Framework

The unturned photo

Hung over my mind
Like tinsel in the palms;

Iterations of everything else
                    superfluous.

Wooden arrows and dried blood
Shelved with the mysterious
                    pieces.

Coffee Mugs
and Lava Lamps

I picked a piece of porcelain
Out of my shoulder today;

It reminded me
How far I've come.
Little slivers
From a fight years ago.

Those shards are nothing more
Than the physical manifestation
Of the internal scars from the years
Of tunneling shame and regret.

Shards indagating what muscles
Look like from the inside.

I save each one
In a little box
So I can throw them
In your face

If you ever show up here.

Gentle Gestures

The smiling faces of today,
In a place where time
Is measured by
The time elapsed since
                someone died,

Were reassuring.

An avalanche
Of events would defile
That reckless simp town.
Months felt like years
And every memory is
Grey-washed and frigid.

Thinking back
Paints overcast skies
Around each structure

And makes me want to
Turn off the AC.

Sweating is hope to me.
Sweating is life to me.
Sweating means I'm free.

Told You It Wouldn't Stop

An anole ran
Across the lawn,
Shuffling blades of grass
To the left and right
As it scuddled through
Like a miniature dinosaur.

Alice called
About an hour prior
Because she was upset
That I couldn't control
Her vibrator while she
Was driving on acid
Because she didn't have WIFI.

Truly the woman of my dreams.

Scuddle your way here
And let me melt into your eyes
Like Electric Sunshine
Straight from the vile.

Shopping Bag Tumbleweeds

Today, my grumbling stomach
Woke me just before sunrise.

I hadn't been able to eat much
In the last few weeks and
I don't know if I can today.
Worst of all, the Beast is
Running low on food, as well.
First article on my phone
Read: '*Poetry is Dead.*'

I rubbed my eyes and took
A resin hit from the bowl,
Took out my pad and pen
And started to write to
Combat such depressing things.

Because, here's the thing:
We're already living the path
We dream of living already.
We are the Beatnik's of
Our generation and the
Only thing dying is creativity.
We already are our own Basquiat,
Our own Ginsberg, our own Kerouac.

Do you think that when Kerouac
Got done working in
The strawberry fields and
Was laying in a janky tent at night,
Next to a woman he loved
But knew he had to leave
The next day,
That he knew college students
Would be discussing his work
30, 40, 50 years after
His stomach last grumbled?

Do you think that when Ginsberg
Was writing epic poems of life,
And love, and fear, and
The beauty of it all,
That he was writing it for

The people of 2020?

Do you think that when Basquiat
First took over SAMO
That his paintings and
Street poetry would live
Forever in infamy?

Or were they just living,
And creating, and writing,
And making, because they can't
Turn it off?

Did their stomachs hurt
Different than ours?
Did they not have the same problems
And live through the same things?

The next time
You can't pay your bills,
The next time
You feel like dying,
The next time
You feel like giving up,
Grab your pen.
Grab your paint.
Grab your precociousness.

'*Poetry is dead,*'
They said, and is
Continually dying…
But here we are;
The last of the poets and artists.
The last of the freethinkers.
The last of the oddballs and outcasts.

And this leaves history
No choice but to discuss us.
And in the same breath
That history can't speak of
Kerouac without mentioning
Ginsberg, Cassady, and Burroughs,
History will have no choice
But to mention Buynak,
Nolasco, Ligeti, and Smith,
And you, and you, and you,
Right alongside icon303.

Think about that the next time
Your stomach growls echo
In empty kitchen cabinets,
The next time your card declines,
Or the next time your
Car breaks down on the highway;

We are already legends,
We may never live to see it…
But we are already
Immortal.

Wild Things

Florida is where
The wild things live.
The grow and thrive
And eat and scavenge.
There's really nothing
You can do to tame it.
Just let them all be,
Furlongs of wild things.

Ego Death 2

I learned not only am I,
But so is my consciousness,
Am/is nothing more than
A drop in the ocean of
Universal consciousness.

Chosen Abulia

I heard you,
I just can't think
Of the right words
To say that quick.
Give me time to
Formulate words,
                    words.

I could move,
But what's the point?
The same thing
Will happen over
Across the room.
Give me some
Encouragement to move,
                    move.

I could make plans,

I just don't trust
Any of you fucks.
Look at where we are.
Partially because
Empathy is lost,
                lost.

Pizza Stops Never

I think we can all agree
That pizza delivery people
Are gods dressed
In commoner's clothing.

Sensibilities

Fuckin hell, I forgot to
Turn off the stove again.
That seems to be a
Common thread in my life.
She says she wants to get
A master's in social work
But ran away after I told her
A story about smoking DMT.
Came back into the stove
Still burning bright red
Like I never turned it off.
I keep doing it, I thought
As I watched her walk
Back to her car and leave.
Maybe if I go stick my hand
Directly on the burner
I'll finally learn to turn it off.

Backyard Broadcasts

Two palms swayed
Looking at each other,
Growing up in the
Same back yard.

One sipped slow
The nutrients that
Scatter the base;
Only when needed.

The other guzzled
And couldn't get
Enough satiation;
Fiending more.

Maybe there was
A board nailed
In his side but

It's an excuse.

Just an excuse
To hang out
With himself
All day.

Memories

She made me feel
Like grass on the
First warm dawn
                    of spring.

And maybe that's
Bound to happen
Abound the treasure map
                    to Eden.

But it sure is a long journey
              on the path
To endless gardens of happiness;
Incantations with fruit
Dripping serotonin and dopamine.

You also stop looking at your gun

as an enemy
with such isolation...

More like
A kissable quiet.
Yeah, that's it,
A kissable quiet.
A romantic,
French kiss
With silence
In the hereafter.

An escape with two cushions
Beckoning in the new shades
Of black and more black
And just shhhhhhhhh.
No more dewed grass
And thick jungles,
Or digging up a chest
Of shit I'll have to hawk.

Not even a goddamn
                    cricket.

Just shhhhh.

Lesson

Things I've learned in Florida:

Dog drool,
Tile floors,
And my feet
Do not mix.

Dear Vanessa,

You should be here
Instead of fuckin'
With those lames.

Obligatory

He must've
Wanted to die
Because his gun
Was out but
Pointed at the ground.

Dance with the witch
And be the nightmare, swine.

I don't see anything
But a walking, talking wound
That never took the time to scarify.

Soaked in the ground
Were his last thoughts,
His hopes and dreams,
And the last bit of love
He had for the rest of us.

It wasn't much fun
Digging it all up,
Or throwing it in the pond
And seeing the bubbles rise.

I either care too much
        or care too little,

        and sometimes even I
        can't decipher
        between the
        two.

Fall, Little Coconut

I sit here
Under this palm,
Watching coconuts fall,
Thinking that

      I'll

         Never

            Forget

               About

                   The

               Time

            You

         Tried

      To

Send

     Me

        To

           A

                          War
                                    In
                    Iraq
               I'd
          Never
     Believe
In.

I'll never forget
Sitting there,
Coming down off heroin,
Trying to plan out a way
To pay for all 4 wisdom teeth
To get extracted
Before the infection
Reached my brain.

But, what's it
To you?

Sand Therapy

I lounge here on the beach
Some days,

Toes only buried
Half as deep in the sand
As my brain in thought.

I stare out over the wave break
And try to imagine you sitting here
                              next to me.

I keep trying to tell myself
That this is it, this is the time
I look over and boom!
There you are...

But unfortunately,
That level of telekinetic power

Is hard to procure.

I want you to know
It wasn't your fault.

I'm sorry.

Deactivate?

Do you ever
Feel towards the world
How you feel
About social media
And spend most the day
Contemplating
Deleting your account,
Or is that
Just me?

Sweet Tea

Life is sweet now.
We must raid
The taco truck
To make it better.

Loop Loop Loop

Maybe anywhere
And everywhere
Is just
Another place
To escape.

In that loop,
It makes me wonder
What I'll do
Once I
Actually
Make it out.

Maybe if
You're in
Pandora's box
It'd be
Insulting to

Ever be
Let out.

In that loop,
It makes me wonder
What I'll ever do
Anywhere and
Everywhere I
Escape.

Moonrat

And when I woke up
In the wet sand-
Just out of reach
Of the tide-

I stood up and whispered
A poem that was meant for
The sand and the sand only.
I pointed myself south,

And walked back between
The edge of the world
And the mansions I'll never
Get a chance to even step

Inside of.

Moon rays dancing off

The rising tide charge me
And urge continuation
Into the near future

When the Beast has
One paw on my arm.
It's the type of
Dual comfortability

Nature offers in four legs
And round nightlights;
A warm blanket with
Fuzzy tassels and lots of

Security.

Trepidation

While the vicious farming technics
                         get some sun.
It won't kill.
          It won't kill.
                    It won't kill.

Hail to the past,
I hate what
I've watched you
Turn into.

Came here to stay but to you,
                         there:
It's home still.
          It's home still.
                    It's home still.

Sunlight to my eyes

Is like feedback
From the speakers.
Bang 'em loud
Outside the lines and praise

oxidation.

It's trepidation.
It's trepidation.
It's trepidation.

Sun-showers

Doom is always
Around the corner
But we just have
To make it through
The 3 pm showers.

Cousins

The sound of
Your snores
Next to me
At 4 am,
As I
Find out that
Amber Heard
Is the
Abuser
And, most likely,
Direct kin
To Carole Baskin,
Is straight
Music.

Commuter

It was supposed to be
An opulent area,
But there was only one
Free park bench
To sit on for miles.

Since when do you
Catch the train on time
And get it to yourself?
How often does
Reggaeton randomly play
In your neighborhood?

The horn honked
And we're away.
My feet are too sweaty
And my heels too
Blistered to walk.

I felt the rails grind
Under the big steel boxes;
Wondering what it did
In its life to
Deserve such weight.

Maybe only an hour
From home and a cool shower.
The Beast awaits me
Just as the dirt will
Tomorrow's sunrise.
Maybe I need to
Take a day off from
Shaping stairs for
Someone else.

Palms tried to
Claw their way
Inside the train
To have a seat
From all the standing.
The bridge over was
Way better than
The bridge back
Due to hope.

Last call for that

Was hours ago
When they warned you
To stand clear of the door.

Make sure you also stand clear
Of the two god fanatics
In front of you.
They're going to talk
About *God* and the devil,
Sins and viruses, misinformation,
And how "it's all men's fault,"
And everything else
"Is a miracle."

The only miracle
Is the joyous lack
Of racism and hatred forthwith
This old White woman
And her new Black friend.
"You have got to go
To Aldi's for the vegetables.
A-and the chicken
Is only two dollars...
Right across the US-1,
By the casino."

Maybe I should steal
That "report graffiti" sign
And replace it with some
Actual graffiti,
And then hang the
Report sign on the casino
And report it.

Last call for Boca Raton,
As Boca Raton has been
For so many generations of elites.
Sadly, I can't wait
To hear last call
For Delray Beach,
Even though it's the
Glycerin overflow
From the boiled fat
Just due south.

<u>Shilling</u>

Leaves tremble
And tremble
While blocking
       the sun

       and here I am,
Aiming my gun,
Hoping it'll point me
In the right direction.

A sugar coat
To stop oxidation
And preserve sheen
Can really help
With everything outside.

We used to
Walk down

Market Street,

but now there's
Just an old lady
Wandering up and down
Asking each person

If they're her son.

Kerouac

We're just
Two poets
Sitting at
        the boardwalk,

The tide and sun
And breeze bring
Our conversations
Of the future new life,
                freshness.

Conversations of the
After and whether or not
We'll be remembered.
And of course,
We will and probably
Mostly for the energy
That's expelled when

You mix chemicals.

Our futures probably
Take pause looking back
At today, right now,
           as I write this.

These times are
The hard ones
We should cherish
       and warble at.

Mary Jane

Weed is
Godmother
Spirit fucks.

Behind the Curtain

Crisp light, crisp light,
Leaking through the shades.

What a ray of change
To the otherwise dim and dingy.

Sweep over the counters
And half-eaten apple cores.

Behind the curtain lies
Sand scree and palm prongs.

Gecko, Gecko

Hopping down to eat
Only an ant, a fly.
Stars are just holes
Poked in the lid
For fresh air.

Siren-Type Alarm

Nothing like
Day old coffee
When I wake up
To piss me off enough
To take on the police.

Only the madman
Would dare,
But it's been
Far too long,
With far too little solved.

Solved…
What a joke
That'll be
When they learn
The answer is
The same thing

I've said since
High school.

Shut it down.
            Abolish.
                Rebuild.
                    Reform.

Azul Convolution

Blue swirl, blue swirl
Of your eyes
As they pass, they pass
Make me cry
Make me laugh.

Just an *azul* convolution,
A cool undulation,
Passerby bloviation,
With the color of her eyes
Lofting by with the wind.

Blue swirl, blue swirl
Of your eyes
As they pass, they pass
Make me cry
Make me laugh.

No cadence or rhythm
Just random seismisms,
A quiet opiumism;
Your love about to ravage

Everything

I knew

About life.

 10 MPH

Swim to see
The wake again
You just dragging
Your finger through
The water creates it.

When you stop moving
Your finger and wait a second
That wake will make way
Into different fields of view.

And if you stay
Stagnant long enough,
There will be no wake
To affect anyone.

Do you want
Your waves lined

With good intentions
And actions or bad;

Do you even
Want wake at all?

Shield

Art acts as a shield
To the outside world
For the artist
In more ways than
Just the psychological ones.

Zootification

We waited in line
And waited in line
For a ride they said
Went faster.

Got tickets an hour ago,
But still can't see the lights.
Maybe there aren't any
Since there's less friction
While running in dark matter.

Finally, it's our time,
Fucking finally our time,
For the sweetest taste
Of the latter.

My Backyard

"It's only Sunday,"
That palm tree told me,
"It's definitely going
To be a good day."

It kept talking,
But I just
Walked past
A group of cops
With a pound of weed
And a loaded handgun
In my backpack.
It takes balls and a poker face,
No eye contact and a steady pace.

And with that,
Shivers of
DMT's past

Run up my spine-
Urging me
To purge
The little
Wonderful ball
Of stress
Welling up
In my solar plexus
Every time I remember
That fuckin palm tree,
THAT FUCKIN PALM TREE!

That palm tree died
Two fuckin weeks ago,
And now,
I'm a bit more worried
Than I was before.

What if I
Never came back
Last Tuesday and
I'm still
Just sitting
In my backyard?

Meet Your Hero

I made you take
A picture at the
Long kitchen table
Under John Lennon's gaze.

My homie,
How can I say
You saved me
In a different way?

I sat with my hero today,
A true living legend.
In a way it saved us both
Because there were words
That needed to be said,
But more importantly heard.

The curse of the artist

Doesn't have to affect you,
I hope you know...
Just like being a good,
Loving, lost artist, husband
All at the same time.

We aren't the pieces of shit
Our dads made us out to be
And our mothers left us for.
We will always have
A side-eye in store
For the rest of the world.

Cheers.

Madlands #4

I've watched my friends
Eat and drink themselves
To death,
Overdose, shoot
And hang themselves,
Or wreck cars...

And I wonder why
It had to be me
Left here looking for jewels
To remind me
That we all once
Had much different
Lives and smiles.

I wonder how
It came to be
That the sediment

That doesn't
Go down the drain
From dirty bath water
Populated
So many hills
In Upstate New York.

Breadcrumbing

I do, you won't
I do, you won't
That's why we're failing.

Jordan

I'm just a dog
On a track,
Chasing a rabbit
I'll never catch.

I've known that
Since I was five years old,
And a psychic told my mom
I was going to be
My own boss.

Run Away from Me

Maybe my pain is
What you need
To love me.

It's played out
Like Don Quixote,
Played out like
The noises my
Shoulder makes
While trying to
Scratch my back.

My physical morality
Has set in and
It's quite wearing
On my mental.

It's played out

Like the Phantom,
Played out like
The opera my heart
Sings every time
You leave me.

Isle of Capris

You can't convince me
There isn't a time machine
Straight to hell in the
Bottom of a bottle.

Nor can you convince me
That there's other ways
Out of the matrix besides
That of the tab on my tongue

right now.

Mostly because,
Anything you say is
Biased to begin with
And can't be trusted.

Maybe one day,

But until that happens,
I'll trust the pieces of paper
That melt the walls right

       in front of me.

Testing, Testing

When I die,
I want no tears
At my funeral.
Only funny stories
Are to be told
On the day I die.

And when I die,
I want all the friends
I have left at the burial,
Or ceremony, or whatever
And wherever,
To light joints in unison.
Everybody at once
And all weed,
No tobacco knock offs,
Or CBD bullshit.
I will haunt you.

Afterward,
I'm going to need everyone
To take 2 tabs of acid each
And sit around a fire
In my backyard.

Love whatever beast I have,
And give whatever books
I have published
To my daughter.

Give all my notebooks
To Ryan Buynak,
And give him the password
To my hard drives,
So he can continue
To publish me posthumously.

After he is done
With the useable material,
I ask he gives
Everything else appropriate
To my daughter.

This is not only my

Last will and testament,
But also, a test
To see if anyone
Actually reads
My poetry.

Trigger Point

I can feel the THC molecules
Expand in my lungs
While I wait for you to
Appear at my door.
Maybe a little more,
Maybe a little more.

I'm a slave to your allure,
Checking the chains are tight
With your good morning texts.
I'll stay despite the
Slop you feed me.
Maybe a little more,
Maybe a little more.

It's a good thing
We can't see the future
Because tomorrow morning

Is going to be hell.
Maybe I can, and that's why
My favorite color is red.
I'll just sleep,
Maybe,
A little more.

Moi?

Buy my tab,
You fuckin prick,
And then I'm done with you.

Library in Paris

I wake up most mornings now
To random toys from the Beast
On the bedroom floor.
I look at them and wonder
What else I would throw
Off the top of the *Centre Pompidou.*
That list would probably
Be made up of mostly my writing
And a few friends' books.

We're too good for refinement,
Life has already refined
And polished our words
To reach a wider audience
When chucked off top
Of elegant structures anyways.

Can you blame us?

When was the last time
You slept under a bridge,
Or lost absolutely everything?
That's just a Sunday for us,
We expect it, at this point.

What can someone
Who has never scrapped a knee
Tell me about life?

The way I see it:
Let those pampered authors
Stay sheltered on their
Climate-controlled bookshelves
While we fly in the skies,

       way

          beyond

             reach.

Up Powell Hill

With Hope there is love
In fifteen seconds
Sitting in a chair,
Giggling at her chins.

I go back once in awhile
And watch just to smile,
And think of a time
You were all mine.

I wish you were here,
To love every fifteen seconds,
Siting in a chair,
Giggling at your chins.

Because, I'll never go back.
Maybe, a day just to pack,
And leave most found

Facing the ground.

Meet me at the gatehouse
In fifteen seconds,
So we can sit in your chair
And giggle at your chins.

Under the X

We were the birthed heirs
To the throne of arts;
A generation of
Disdained creators to balk
About the sins of the father.

There is no weather here,
Just sweat equity and sorrow.
No jewels behind iron locks
And no gold bullion.

Worst of all:
No map leading us
To where that shit is, either.
Not even a hint.

I have a feeling
It's close to where

The dunes mirror the waves,
Crashing into themselves
Like the journey
Just undertook.

Dabman Cometh

On a day when I need you most
And anxiety is high,
Where were you hiding,
Where were you hiding?

GPS says 27 minutes,
But it's not accounting
For hellish Florida traffic.

How am I to survive
This day posed to
Be the most perfect day?

On a day when I need you most
And anxiety is high,
You're almost here
You're almost here.

The Beast sniffs the corner
Of my front door upon arrival,
And I instantly feel better.

Come on in and chill
For a couple hours
And talk some shit.

On a day when I need you most
And anxiety is high,
You saved me,
You saved me.

Tree Shadow Cadence

The reflection of my shadow
Dances in the sand
While the waves clap a cadence
Leading the rhythm to you.
See it dance in the sand
And the footprints wash away
After my soul left the scene.
Watch my soul wash away
After the waves clap the cadence.
See it dance to the
Reflection of my shadow as it
Waves to the rhythm of you.

I just want to grow into a tree
And donate more shadows
To an ever-sunny soul.
Let the wind rattle the leaves
Like a tambourine to the

Beat of the rhythm of you.
All the roots help to
Watch them fall away
And land in the shade,
Below all the gusts of sun,
Donated from a tree
My soul rattled to growth.

Pre-Prohibition Yak

The dishwasher
Whirling away
In the background
Made me want
To try 1913
Legal cocaine.

Partook

I see you,
Opening presents
In glee

With your friends
On zoom and
Family gathered.

Look at the
Things I got!
Just what I've
Always wanted!

But I'll never be
Uncle, cousin,
Or daddy.

I'll never be

Brother, friend,
Or grandpa.

I'll never be
Love, husband,
Or son.

See, I was once
And it was ripped away.

And it's still hard to heal.

I sat this Christmas
Just the Beast and I.
We watched movies that
Had nothing to do with
The current holiday.
No decorations, no music.
No movies, no reminders

That I'll never be
Uncle
Cousin
Brother
Friend
Love
Husband

Son
Daddy
Grandpa

Tropical Depression

I'm waiting on a certain dove
From the Madlands
To land in my palm trees.
Waiting for her to swoop in
And save the night with
Concerts of orchestral chirps
And rainbow plumage
Decorating the horizon.
Waiting for her to greet me
In the morning when
I bring out the Beast and tea.
Waiting for her to
Sit on my shoulder
While I write about nothing.

Sadly, I think this cold front
Is moving in and that will
Confuse the migration a bit.

I don't think she expects
The overcast skies
And storm brewing off the coast.
Hopefully the tropical depression
Decides whether it wants
To blow its fuckin head off or not,
Because I cannot bare
Another songless morning
And have been stuck
In mourning for far too long.
Maybe she'll wait a day
And miss the cold front altogether
On her trip to the palm tree,
And I'll be here, waiting.

Sun and Shade

The hammock creaked
As it swung me
Between sun and shade,
Sun and shade.

Creaked like my body
When I move about.
The hammock is complaining,
I feel like the hammock
Is asking me to get up.

That is a humbling crossroad
To be have stumbled upon.
Its disarming to think
Something that's only purpose
Is to let you lay in it,
Wants you to get out,
Creaking in pain.

You little fabric,
Tinselly piece of shit,
You wouldn't be here
If people didn't need to lay in you.
But still it winced
The entirety of me resting.

Then it dawned on me,
I'd creak if someone stopped me
From swaying in the wind,
Dancing to the rhythm emotions
In the sun and shade,
Sun and shade.

I'd creak if everyone thought
My only purpose was
To rest their feet,
To use me to take a load off.
I'd creak if I was only needed
When someone else needed.

A villain, am I not,
Taking away the life,
The vibrance of a free soul
Dancing in elation?
A narcissist that only sees

What you can do for me,
Never what that means for you.
A vile excuse from English,
The same type of conundrum
In the language that allows you
To say, "I need you,"
And through a samba with tonality,
Still not mean it;
The words passing
Through sun and shade,
Sun and shade.

Corner Store Love

I got up and took a walk
Through the hood.
I could smell the weed burning,
The sprinklers on pavement,
And lawns being cut.
I gave a bunch of stickers away
To the dudes smokin' a blunt
On the way to the store.

They thought I was a crackhead.
I said, "Naa, just a starving artist.
These stickers are for me, bro.
I stay up the block."
They took them and hopefully
Put them everywhere.
I saved my book
For the homeless man
I see reading on the corner every day

And gave him a signed copy.
Maybe something in there
Can help or give some hope.

These are my days now,
Such a far cry from the
Heroin days in Harlem.
No more watching for
Undercovers in parked cars
And running from places
We shouldn't be.
No more lying to probation officers
About where I'm staying
Or crossing state lines
Without permission
With 100 stamps of heroin,
2 eight-balls of coke,
2 ounces of weed
Bagged up in eighths,
An unregistered handgun,
2.5 of a 5-year
Felony probation sentence,
Both drivers nodding out
From the heroin while driving
And crossing into other lanes,
And a 4-hour trip home ahead of us.

Now, I just give my books
To the people who need them most
And make art only
A few will understand.
I give stickers to dudes chillin'
At a table on a sunny,
South Florida afternoon.
And for this,

I'm thankful.

BE

Weird enough
To weird out
The weirdos.

Six Flags

Grieving is the worst
Rollercoaster of life,
With your hopes
And dreams ready
To be puked all over
The next shmuck.

Luckily, he's was
A few carts back
And can't reach you.

But when the carts
Come to a halt
And the people
In front of you
Are done puking too,

You get subpoenaed

For family court.
Just let me grieve,
You bastards…
Just let me grieve.

Beast Longing

There she was,
Watching the door
For the friend
That would never
Come back.

Vanquished

I see these scenes
Of people leaving
Their home for stardom
And their families
Send them off
With loving praise
And their friends all
Gathering.

Mine was rather silent.
Nobody heard me leave
Or wished me *"Bon voyage."*
Nobody said they were
Going to miss me.
Nobody hugged me
Or fucked me one last time.

I just left.

Disappeared.
Vanished.
Reclused myself
To myself
And myself only.

Most of you didn't
Deserve to know me
To begin with,
Let alone stay
For any prolonged time.

I'd rather it that way.

Partyman

I miss the days
With raging parties
And no masks
Or party control.

I miss hearing
Prince's *Partyman*
Jam in the land of
No rules and regulations.

I miss the days
I could invite someone over
Without Lysol and distance
And total awkwardness.

But these are the days
And they're far from over.
Too many people think

It's a hoax for control.

And trust me,
I'm all about
Conspiracy theories,
But ones that make sense.

Just do us a favor
And wear a damn mask.
Partyman, Partyman
No place in this nation.

R.I.P.
Prince Rogers Nelson

Fall

The leaves
Have all but
Shed in a show
Of dignity
And fortitude.

Canvas ~~Easily~~ Painted

I watched the sun rise
Over some palms with a
Drizzling sun shower today.

It was alluring to watch
A pastel-colored cleanse
Of last night and the things
Better left forgotten.

Yellows and greens
And lavender are there
To remind me that
Gripes go up.

If the blues weren't so beautiful,
I'd fail to mention them at all…
But how could I not?

The blistering cool and cold
Of the icy blue haze that
Daunts my every angry motive;
The peace and solidarity it brings
To the morning's
Good morning to us all.

A little rain for the
Water-colored aurora
To accentuate the narrative
For the rest of the day.

"The soul is a treasure chest;

hidden inside of it are

priceless jewels."

-Matshona Dhliwayo